Weather Wisdom
. . . fact or fiction?

by Ron Lobeck

Published by
Geerings of Ashford Limited

To Raymond
Best wishes
Ron Lobeck
26. April 1989

Red sky at dawning . . . does it mean rain . . . ?

Illustrations and photographs
by the Author (with exceptions)

Acknowledgements

My thanks to the following for allowing
me to include some of their photographs:

Kent Messenger Group
John Gotts; Pamela Lobeck
Roger Nicholson; Mrs. S. Rycroft
Peter Smith; Cliff Wyatt

. . . and not forgetting Paul Smith for
providing the introduction to Robert Geering
who has given me the chance . . .

Weather Lore

"Birds and bees . . .
. . . or talk to the trees . . ."

Weather lore is a part of man's heritage.
Since the dawn of creation, every
culture has sought to connect nature's
signs and subsequent weather patterns,
in an attempt to produce a forecast system.

Looking at the many sayings that have developed it is apparent that they tend to divide into two main sections.

One group relies on observation of prevailing conditions, such as state of the sky, wind direction, sun haloes, while the other concerns the behaviour of animals, birds, insects and plant life; for example cows' lying . . . cats' licking . . . gnats' biting, not forgetting the much beloved seaweed and ever faithful fir cone.

If I had to offer an opinion as to which of the two groups was likely to provide a more accurate forecast, I would select the first, for the simple reason that it might be difficult to find a particular animal, bird or insect at a specific time; a bit like policemen: ". . . you can never find one when you want one . . .!"

On the other hand, the sky, clouds and wind are much more in evidence and you do not have to live in the country in order to observe them.

Most of the forecasts derived from weather lore are 'long range', that is they attempt to predict the weather for days, weeks or even months ahead.

By their very nature (excuse the pun) they usually depend upon a single observation and are unlikely to be updated for some considerable time.

Modern weather forecasts are short term and they are frequently updated.

The computer generated products, which are based upon mathematical models of the atmosphere, rarely extend more than seven days ahead. Those forecasts with which we are most familiar, such as the ones presented upon Radio and TV cover only the next 24 hours, but they are modified about every six hours. The whole idea is to keep up to date with weather changes over a wide geographical area by means of regular hourly observations. It is these observations that provide the basic information upon which the forecast is issued.

Thus the content of a forecast can change radically as time progresses, a fact that sometimes irritates the user. For example, at mid-day he may be told that the next day will be dry and mostly sunny. A few hours later, an updated forecast, based on fresh observations, now predicts the onset of rain early the next day. Since the predicted rain will interfere with his plans, he becomes resentful and offers the opinion that the forecasters " . . . cannot make up their minds . . ." The fact that the rain does arrive, as forecast, carries little weight.

1

It is, therefore, easy to see the attraction of weather lore. In the depths of a cold gloomy winter, the prospect of a warm Spring, followed by a hot summer is particularly inviting, and if there is an old saying that suggests the dream might become reality, how eagerly it is accepted.

What chance does a seven day forecast that predicts the cold weather will persist have against such a beacon of hope?

Not that forecasts based on weather lore only predict fair weather ahead. There are many sayings that prophesy storms, floods and other meteorological disasters. Obviously it was very important that our forefathers were warned of impending bad weather, especially as their life styles made them more vulnerable than nowadays, as the Bible describes . . .

". . . For He says to the snow, 'Fall to earth', and to the rainstorms 'Be fierce.' . . .
. . . the floods of rain pour down unchecked. He shuts every man fast indoors . . .
and all . . . must stand idle . . . the beasts withdraw into their lairs . . ."   *Job 37*

The day to day weather variations are less important to western man. Collectively and individually we are becoming more detached from our environment. Central heating, double glazing, mass transit systems and the motor car all provide an effective barrier to the daily weather. Even our clothing is designed to significantly reduce the effects of the weather. It seems only those violent extremes that occasionally happen have any large impact on our lives and those are often the most difficult to forecast.

Therefore, is there any place for weather lore in the modern world?

The honest answer is, I think: yes, but only for those sayings that are based on the recognition of the definite changes that take place in our atmosphere when certain weather patterns are developing.

I firmly believe that anyone who spends their working life out of doors and whose livelihood depends on the impact of the weather, if they are reasonably intelligent they will develop the ability to read the signs and interpret them to produce short term forecasts for their own locality.

It is in this way that, over the centuries, weather lore has built up amongst farmers and fishermen that does give sensible results.

Other sayings, however, appear to have no basis in the physical world whatsoever and seem to be pure whimsy.

In the following pages you will find examples of both types so that you can test their truth or falsehood.

There may be sayings familiar to you that are not quoted. It might be that you feel these sayings actually work, if so: good for you!

However, it is worth remembering that the time scale is often very large and what appears to work one year may not always be the case.

At the same time, why not look and listen a little more carefully to the day to day forecasts and see how they perform, but please, always listen to, or read, the most up to date available.

Remember, Benjamin Franklin said:

"Some are weatherwise, Some are otherwise"

Origins

We have already seen that the Bible refers to the effects the weather had on the livelihood of man and his animals. It also has many vivid descriptions of the extremely variable weather conditions that can occur in that part of the world, depending upon the season.

Violent thunderstorms with lightning and hailstones plus severe squalls are often mentioned and the causes are usually attributed to the 'wrath of God'.

This is understandable since at that time there was ignorance concerning the physical processes that occur in the atmosphere when such storms are brewing.

However, not all the comments upon the weather are lacking in understanding.

For example, in the Book of Job, we find Elihu, son of Barakel, and what he has to say shows a very good insight into weather processes . . .

"Look up at the sky . . . observe the rain clouds towering above you . . ."

he told Job, and then went on . . .

> *"He draws up drops of water from the sea and distils rain from the mist he has made; the rain clouds pour down in torrents, they descend in showers . . ."*

which shows a remarkable understanding of what is now called the 'Water Cycle'.

This means that the sun's heat causes evaporation of water (liquid) into water vapour (gas). Such a process is taking place all the time over the tropical oceans and seas like the Mediterranean where evaporation is particularly strong in the summer. The water vapour mixes with the air we breathe and on cold days we can see the fine water droplets formed as it condenses on our breath or on a cold window pane. It is the water vapour that gives the air its humidity or moisture content. If the air is forced to rise it cools and the water vapour condenses into droplets which form clouds. If the clouds become thick enough (dense) then rain (or snow) can be precipitated.

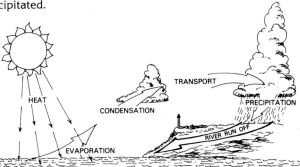

Next Elihu gives a good description of sea fog . . .

> ". . .see how He unrolls the mist across the waters and its streamers
> cover the sea." . . .

followed by thunderstorms, with an accurate account of the violent gusts of cold
air that can be associated with the sudden onset of heavy rain . . .

> . . . "The hurricane bursts from its prison and the rain winds bring bitter
> cold . . ."

Remarkable falls in temperature often take place with a summer or autumn
thunderstorm, especially in the eastern Mediterranean.

An awareness of upper winds and their role in the transport of moisture is also
indicated . . .

> ". . . He gives the dense clouds their moisture and the clouds spread his
> mist abroad, as they travel . . . all over the habitable world . . ."

Finally, Elihu concludes with comments on the seasonal winds that prevail
over the Middle East . . .

> ". . . sweating there . . . when the earth lies sultry under the south wind
> . . ."

The south winds have their origins over the deserts of the Sahara or Saudi
Arabia and as a result they are hot, dry and very enervating. They develop ahead
of depressions that move eastwards over the Mediterranean. They are known as
the *sirocco* or *khamsin* depending upon the region.

In the gospel according to Luke the heat of the south winds is also recognised . . .

> ". . . and when the wind is from the south you say it will be hot, and it
> is . . ."

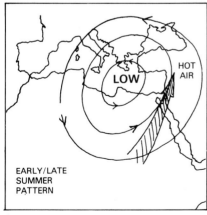

EARLY/LATE
SUMMER
PATTERN

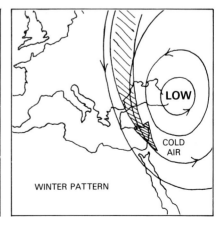

WINTER PATTERN

Mediterranean sunrise . . .

The east wind is associated with extreme dryness, or cold and could be very strong. In the Book of the Prophet Ezekiel we find . . .

> ". . . the east wind blighted it, its fruit was blown off, its strong branches blighted . . ."

and . . .

> "Will it not be utterly shrivelled, as though by the touch of the east wind . . .?"

Jonah not only had to contend with life inside the belly of a fish but he had to suffer the effects of the east wind . . .

> ". . . a scorching wind should blow up from the east. The sun beat down on Jonah's head so he grew faint . . ."

Hot dry east winds would be a feature of low pressure systems centred over Saudi Arabia or north west India.

In winter a bitter east wind would be generated by high pressure centred over south Russia and it could give gales, which would explain the following comments . . .

> "Ships of Tarshish . . . on the high seas . . . an east wind wrecked you . . ." Ezekiel 27

The same incident is mentioned in Psalm 48 . . .

> ". . . destroyed like ships of Tarshish . . . by an east wind . . ."

Whilst in the Bible, north, east and south are all associated with various winds, the west is the region from which showers are predicted to develop as we find in Luke . . .

> "When you see a cloud banking up in the west, you say at once, 'It is going to rain' and rain it does . . ."

In the First Book of Kings Elijah issues one of the earliest weather forecasts when he orders his servant to look out to the west. Seven times he gives the instruction and finally the servant reports . . .

> ". . . I see a cloud no bigger than a man's hand, coming up from the west . . ."

Whereupon Elijah orders Ahab to be off. . .

> ". . . or the rain will stop him . . ."

Roger Nicholson

". . . lightnings are loosened . . ." (Browning)

Then follows a very good description of a thunderstorm.

Actually just before he gave Ahab the forecast, Eijah made a very interesting point . . .

". . . I hear the sound of coming rain . . ."

Now it may be that he heard the far off thunder, however, the idea that the propagation of sounds can be an indicator of impending weather conditions occurs often in weather lore.

Such a notion may well have some merit because the speed of sound waves in the lower atmosphere can be affected by meteorological conditions.

The most obvious of which is wind, the speed and direction having a marked effect on how any noise will travel from its source to the listener.

It is a fact that as certain weather systems develop the wind changes direction and often increases in speed. This is particularly true when depressions are approaching.

Other factors that have an effect on sound propagation are air temperature and humidity or moisture content. An increase in either causes a rise in the speed of sound, in the lower levels of the atmosphere.

Again these two parameters often increase at the same time, usually when a depression is on its way with its band of bad weather.

So the suggestion that because certain sounds are suddenly clearly audible, such the noise from a distant railway or waves on a shingle beach, the weather is likely to deteriorate and rain appear is not without some scientific basis.

7

A nice example of such a belief is the noise of the so called 'Bulverhythe Bells'. Fishermen in the Hastings area on the English Channel coast say that when they can hear the sounds of the beach waves raking the shingle at Bulverhythe to the west, then bad weather will approach from the west.

As low pressure systems move east into the Channel, the winds pick up from the southwest, aiding the transmission of sounds to the east.

Also with the vigorous storms a heavy swell is generated and this moves quickly ahead of the centre. Such a swell moving up the English Channel would be expected to generate heavy beach waves thus increasing the noise level.

But back to our look at Biblical weather.

There are many passages that describe weather phenomena, ranging from the great flood in Genesis to the parting of the Red Sea in Exodus. This latter is nowadays explained in terms of tide and wind.

It has been suggested that the children of Israel crossed the Red Sea to the south of the Bitter Lakes, which in biblical times were still connected to the northern part of the Red Sea. A very strong east wind, possibly combined with a region of high pressure, caused an extra low tide, allowing the Israelites to cross. However, as the wind decreased and the tide turned the pursuing Egyptians were caught by the incoming waters.

In the New Testament we find one of the earliest records of what is perhaps the best known saying throughout the world . . .

> "When the sun is setting, you say, 'We are going to have fine weather because the sky is red'. And early in the morning you say, 'it is going to rain because the sky is red and lowering' . . ."

8

". . . Sunsets exquisitely dying . . . " (Aldous Huxley)

Nowadays this expression is . . .

"Red sky at night, Shepherd's delight,
Red sky at morning, Shepherd's warning"

9

It is interesting to note that this version omits the phrase 'and lowering' which is in the biblical prediction. This may explain why the attempt to connect red sky in the morning with approaching rain does not always work.

But why should a red sky at sunset, which is what is meant, be a good indicator of fine weather?

The answer is connected to the question . . . "Why is the sky blue?"

Sunlight or 'white light' is a combination of different colours ranging from red to dark blue or violet. These are the colours of the spectrum and are usually seen in a rainbow.

The rainbow is formed because sunlight on entering a raindrop suffers refraction, that means the rays are bent. The different colours that make up the white light are bent by differing amounts, the red is refracted to a lesser degree than the blue. In this way the white light is separated into the different colours within the raindrop.

Some of these colours are then reflected within the drop whilst others pass through to be further refracted and reflected in an adjacent raindrop.

In this way the separation is enhanced and the light of the different colours arrives at the observer from slightly different angles, giving the rainbow.

Rainbows are usually associated with showers or thunderstorms, but they can be admired anywhere there are water drops floating in the air, such as at waterfalls or in the spray of the garden hose.

In order to see a rainbow clearly we have to have the sun at our backs. This gives rise to a variation of the traditional rhyme . . .

Rainbow at night, Shepherd's delight
Rainbow in the morning, Shepherd's warning . . .

As a weather predictor this is somewhat more reliable than the traditional rhyme.

The reason is that, as stated, rainbows are a feature of showery airstreams. In the United Kingdom, western Europe and the Mediterranean, such airstreams are associated with westerly or northwest winds.

Hence, if the rainbow is observed near sunset, the shower must be to the east of the observer and would be expected to move away on the westerly winds.

There is another factor to be considered and that is that away from the westerly coasts, especially in spring or summer, showers are often generated by surface heating. After sunset this dies away and the showers decay, especially inland, so that a dry night follows.

A rainbow in the morning with the sun in the east means that the showers are to the west and likely to approach on the west winds. Also the increasing heating effect of the sun on the ground would help to prolong further showers as the day progressed.

Pamela Lobeck

Evening rainbow　　　　　　　　*. . . Rainbow at Niagara Falls . . .*

Now, in addition to being refracted and reflected within water drops, sunlight is also scattered by particles in the atmosphere. This means that the rays 'bounce off' the molecules in the air plus any fine dust present.

The amount of scattering depends on the colour (wavelength) of the light and the size of the particles. In the atmosphere, when the sun is well above the horizon, the molecules of the air are about six times more effective at scattering the blue light towards the surface than the red, hence, the sky appears blue during the day.

A good example of the favouring of blue light in scattering can be seen in the colour of cigarette smoke. It is actually yellow as can be proved by letting it condense on a white surface or by exhaling the fine mist through a clean handkerchief. However, because of the size of the particles favours the scattering of the blue light, the smoke appears blue. This applies to most smoke particles.

When the sun is low in the sky, as at sunrise or sunset, the light has to pass through a much greater depth of atmosphere and any suspended particles can start to have an effect upon the scattering.

If there is a lot of dust or haze in the lower levels of the air then scattering of the red light is favoured.

The presence of large amounts of dust implies that the air is dry, otherwise any water vapour would tend to condense out on the particles, thus changing their scattering characteristics and altering the red colour.

11

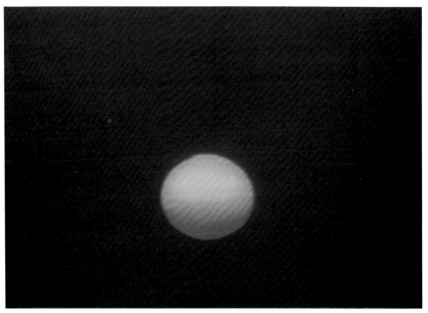

. . . Another fine day to come . . . ?

If the colouration is pronounced at sunset it means that there is dry air to the west and since most of our weather comes from the west, the assumption that the following day will be fine is a reasonable one.

Red sky at dawn means dry air to the east which could mean a fine day if east winds prevailed and if the pressure was steady, and high.

Remember that in the biblical quotation there is the phrase . . .

". . . and lowering . . ."

which may be the reason for the uncertainty that can attach to trying to use " . . . red sky at morning . . ." as a predictor of impending rain.

As the size of the airborne particles increases so their effectiveness as scatterers diminishes.

The sun when viewed through smoke has a reddish tinge but through a cloud or fog bank, it is seen as a white disc or diffuse white spot. This is because at the size of the water droplets that make up the cloud or fog, the scattering effect is negligible.

The effect of clouds comprised of ice crystals will be described in the next section but we end this with the words of Elihu, who not only understood many of the weather processes but also the problems of the forecaster . . .

". . . Can any man read the secret of the sailing clouds? . . ."

"The Greeks had a word for it . . ."

Around 300BC Theophrastus, a greek philosopher and pupil of Aristotle, wrote his "Book of Weather Signs". In which he listed some 200 or so portents of the weather.

Amongst them are many that still survive today, such as the fact that haloes around the sun or moon are usually followed by rain.

These haloes are caused by high level clouds, at heights generally above 20,000ft. At these altitudes the clouds are thin, and made up of ice crystals. The cloud type responsible for the formation of haloes is called cirrostratus.

Rays of sunlight or moonlight filter through the thin cloud layer and some are reflected from the faces of the ice crystals. Other rays pass through the transparent ice and are refracted so the light is separated into the colours of spectrum. In this way the ice crystals act as prisms just like the glass of a crystal chandelier.

The most common halo is the result of refraction and often only a partial curve is seen at a radius of 22 degrees from the sun.

. . . the appearance of the 22° halo is a particularly good indicator of the probability of rain in January and December . . .

When conditions are right, other haloes can be seen as well as related phenomena such as 'Mock Suns'. These appear as bright spots, sometimes looking like shortened rainbows. Amongst old seafarers these were known as 'Sun Dogs' . . .

The sailor takes warning of a sun dog at dawning . . .

This proverb raises some interesting points . . .

The sun rises in the east and since the sun dogs are caused by high level cirrus clouds, for them to be seen at, or just after sunrise implies that the observer is to the *west* of the depression or unsettled weather.

In the temperate latitudes the tendency is for most depressions to move from *west* to *east*. Thus, if the high cirrus is to the east of the observer, then the unsettled weather would tend to move away and the proverb has little value.

However, in lower latitudes, especially the Tropics, bad weather tends to move from *east* to *west*.

Thus, at these latitudes the sun dogs associated with the cirrus clouds could provide useful indicators of a tropical disturbance which often bring sudden violent squalls or even hurricane force winds.

For those in sailing ships such advance warning could be the difference between life and death.

13

. . . Mock Sun or Sundog . . .   See P.16(M)

So it seems that the saying is of value in the Tropics.

One thing to be clear about is the difference between a halo and a corona. The latter is much smaller in diameter and is often seen surrounding streetlights, especially in misty conditions. At times it can be seen around the moon when it is viewed through thin low level clouds.

The corona is formed by water droplets and its presence could indicate a risk of fog or mist if it appears around streetlights.

But why should Theophrastus connect the appearance of haloes with impending rain?

Well, the cirrostratus cloud responsible is most often seen ahead of an approaching warm front, which is a region of bad weather where rain can be heavy. If the air at the surface is cold enough then snow occurs instead of rain.

The cloud structure of a typical warm front shows that the cirrostratus is about 500 miles ahead of the rain bearing clouds, at heights between 20,000ft and 25,000ft:-

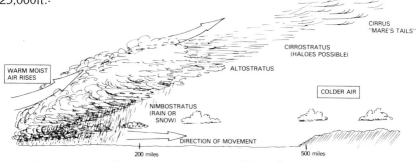

Vertical section through Warm Front

An approaching Warm Front . . .

Cirrus "Mare's Tails"   Cirrostratus

22° Halo formed by Cirrostratus

15

Mock suns are often seen in winter when the sun is low in the sky and are formed at the intersection of the various haloes that can occur as the diagram illustrates . . .

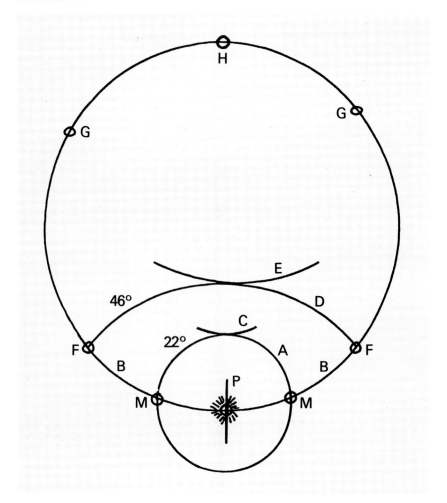

M – Mock suns formed by intersection of 22° halo (A), the parhelic circle (B) known as 'sun dogs' (parhelia)

F – Bright spots formed by intersection of 46° halo (D) and the parhelic circle (B) called parhelia

P – Sun pillars

C – Arc of contact to 22° halo (A)

E – Circumzenithal arc, a rainbow effect

G – Bright spots (paranthelia)

H – The Antihelion, a very bright spot opposite the sun

Circumzenithal Arc (E)
and Arc of Contact (C)

Sun Pillar in Daytime (P)

Cliff Wyatt

Parhelia (F)

Sun Pillar in daytime (P)

17

When we look at the region where Theophrastus and the biblical prophets lived, it is obvious that the weather patterns, particularly in summer, tend to be settled for long periods. The onset of bad weather in the eastern Mediterranean is much more seasonal than in the British Isles. We do not enjoy the luxury of guaranteed long hot summers. To describe our weather as "changeable" is something of an understatement.

Comparing what we get with the eastern Mediterranean and Middle East, it could be said that:

> They get climate,
> We get weather!

The following statements are by Horace Walpole, who was the fourth Earl of Orford, in the 18th century. They demonstrate clearly the British attitude to our weather . . .

In July 1775 during a particularly long hot summer Walpole said:

> *"I believe Joshua has bid the sun stand still, for there has not been a bad day since December."*

However, just two summers later his opinion had changed, in keeping with the weather:

> *"We are in truth Greenlanders and ought to learn to conform to our climate. We should lay in stores of provisions, candles and coloured lamps for ten months of the year, shut out our twilight, and enjoy ourselves."*

So, even more than two hundred years ago the British climate was as inconsistent as it appears to be today.

To paraphrase a well known rhyme . . .

> When it's good, it's very, very good,
> but when it's bad, it's diabolical . . .!

The next collection of sayings are those that purport to predict the weather by means of conditions prevailing during a particular month. Sometimes two or more months are combined to produce a long term prediction . . .

anuary brings the snow
Makes our toes and fingers
glow. . .

. . . Often the coldest month of the year, the very low temperatures are usually caused by biting east winds, which are associated with high pressure centred over Scandinavia or west Russia. The air is not only very cold it is also very dry. However, depending upon its track across the North Sea it can produce heavy snow showers over eastern counties. Once the cold easterlies are established, low pressure systems and their associated fronts, approaching from the Atlantic, tend to become slow moving over Biscay and the southwest approaches. As the warm, moist Atlantic air piles up over the cold, dry, Continental air, snowfall occurs over the southwest peninsula. This snow then tends to move eastwards along the Channel, blanketing southern England, especially as the high pressure starts to relax . . .

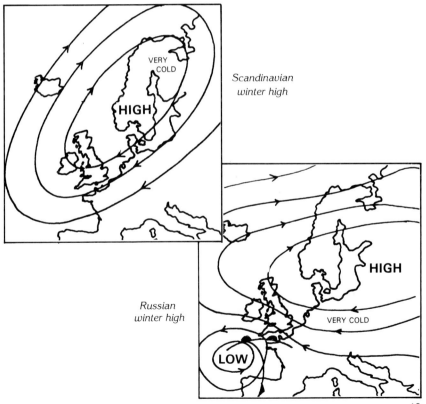

Scandinavian
winter high

Russian
winter high

19

A green winter
makes a fat
churchyard . . .

Mild winters herald
sickly summers . . .

January commits the fault and May bears the blame . . .

. . . In both 1933 and 1937, January was mild and an Influenza epidemic developed with many deaths . .

In 1882, during mild weather, London was gripped by a dense fog which persisted for much of January and resulted in many deaths . . .

*

The first three days of January rule the coming three months . . .

. . . or do they . . ?

In 1947, January opened with three days when the maximum temperature was 7.2C(45F). Then followed a short cold spell, after which the weather turned very mild with temperatures of 12.7C(55F) on the 16th. However, by the 23rd, the worst snowstorms since 1891 blanketed the south. This bitterly cold weather persisted until late March.

In January 1948, it was particularly mild at the start of the month and, apart from 10in. of snow over Kent on 21st February, it remained mild and wet throughout the winter.

However, the weather pattern of January 1947 could be used to support the following . . .

If there is much sun in January, no good we'll see,
for in February and March sure revenge will be . . .

*

Better to see thy mother on a bier than to see fair weather in January . . .

*

These sayings illustrate the strong theme of pessimism that is a feature of much weather lore, especially that connected with mild winters . . .

In Janiveer if the sun appear,
March and April pay full dear . . .

It seems as if our forefathers could not believe their luck when fair weather prevailed in January.

Of course, with the housing and sanitary conditions that existed throughout the middle ages and through to Victorian times, the absence of a hard frost must have favoured the breeding of germs. Prior to the severe winter of 1740, England had suffered several widespread epidemics of smallpox, diptheria and typhoid.

Which probably explains why they were always looking over their shoulders for impending disaster and sudden change . . .

January will strike down . . .

*

January, the blackest month . . .

On the other hand, we could consider what the proverbs say from a different point of view and argue that they lend strong support to the fact that the British climate is extremely variable, especially in the winter season.

The following are a more or less random selection of mild and very cold Januarys. The fact that there are more listed for the better part of the 20th century under the heading 'Mild' should not be taken as evidence that the climate has become milder. It is simply that in the past, very cold Januarys were noted, whereas the mild ones were taken for granted!

VERY COLD	MILD
1572, 1580, 1592,	1662, 1882,
1608, 1684,	1903, 1928, 1933,
1740, 1795,	1937, 1949, 1973,
1814, 1881,	1974, 1975, 1981,
1947, 1963, 1982,	1986, 1988, 1989
1985, 1987	

Stan Rycroft

. . . Deep, crisp and uneven! . . .

Frost Fairs . . .

The last time the River Thames froze within London was in 1814, when the last of the so called 'Frost Fairs' was held.

Other famous occasions were in 1564 when football was played on the ice. During 1607-8 enterprising folk set up booths and lighted fires to roast ox and sheep.

The events were repeated during the very severe winters of 1621, 1684, 1688, 1715, 1739, 1789 . . .

The fairs were always set up between Blackfriars and the old London bridges.

It is suggested that because of its construction, old London Bridge acted like a dam and separated the more saline tidal waters of the estuary from the fresh river water to the west and fresh water freezes much more readily than does salt water.

Notable January Weather . . .

3 Jan 1978	Tornadoes struck Newmarket (Suffolk) causing considerable damage.
7 Jan 1928	River Thames already swollen by rain and melted snow combined with a large spring tide and northerly gale to burst its banks, giving extensive flooding in London with the loss of 14 lives.
14 Jan 1952	Winds of up to 127 mph (203 kph) recorded at Orkney Isles before the apparatus blew away.
31 Jan 1953	Severe North Sea gales brought floods to East Anglia and the low countries with much loss of life.

ebruary brings the rain, Thaws the frozen lake again . . .

. . . On average February is the driest of the winter months. It is often a quiet month with severe frosts or very mild spells. The lowest temperature recorded in the British Isles was at Braemar on 11th February 1895.

. . . Combined with January it gives the coldest two months of the year in Europe . . .

"Russia has two Generals she can trust, Generals January and February"

So said Nicholas 1 of Russia . . . Napoleon Bonaparte and Adolf Hitler would surely agree.

*

All the months of the year curse a fair Februeer . . .

*

When the gnats dance in February,
the husbandman becomes a beggar . . .

*

The concern in this proverb over a mild spell in winter is perhaps derived from the fact that parasites that attack animals, such as the liver fluke and blow fly, would not only survive but would become active earlier in the season. Whereas a good hard frost would tend to kill a lot of them.

If grass grows in February it grows worst for the rest of the year . . .

A mild winter usually means that rainfall is above average and floods result . . .

February fill ditch, March drink ditch . . .

*

. . . and heavy rain is often associated with strong to gale force winds . . .

February blows and gives no rest, It blows the little bird off its nest . . .

*

The weather pattern that brings the snow and bitter weather in January is one that can show remarkable persistence, so the bitter weather often carries over into February . . .

February blows cold, The bird freezes in its nest . . .

23

". . . the secret ministry of frost . . ." (Coleridge)

February 2nd is Candlemas Day and it is mentioned in weather proverbs . . .

An hour of sun on Candlemas Day,
makes the summer dark and grey . . .

*

If Candlemas sees a day of sun,
Half of the winter is yet to come . . .

There does not appear to be an optimistic version, so here's my own . . .

If Candlemas be dull and wet
We'll have a summer we won't forget . . . !

Notable February Weather . . .

February 1947   – Snow covered the whole country for all of the month . . . on the 24th a temperature of – 17C (1F) was recorded at Cambridge . . .

11 Feb 1895   – Temperature fell to – 27.2C (– 17F) at Braemar, Scotland . . .

14 Feb 1948   – Temperature rose to 14.4C (58F) at Defford, Worcester . . .

22 Feb 1948   – At Tunbridge Wells, Kent, the temperature fell to – 14C (7F) and 25cm (10in) of snow fell at Biggin Hill. . .

February 1958 – During the last week heavy snow and winds up to 70 mph (112 kph) hit the southwest of England . . .

arch brings breezes, loud and shrill, to stir the dancing Daffodil . . .

. . . daffodils,
That come before the swallow dares, and take
The winds of March with beauty; . . .
Shakespeare: The Winter's Tale

March is the month of change. It includes the introduction of British Summer Time, which is when the clocks are advanced one hour. For those who have difficulty in remembering whether the clocks go forward or back, the following may help:
"Spring forward —
Fall back"
'Fall' in this sense refers to Autumn.

It is also the month of the Vernal Equinox, which marks the end of 'Official' Winter and the start of 'Official' Spring. The weather often has other ideas!

*

Changeable March . . .

In 1965 temperatures ranged from a low of minus 21.7C (– 7F) on the 3rd, recorded in North Wales, to a maximum of 25.0C(77F) at Wakefield on the 29th.

There is a strong tendency for weather proverbs concerning March, to link it with another month to produce a combined prediction. Already we have seen examples in January and February and there are the following . . .

March will slay, April will flay . . .

March wind and May sunshine will make ugly what should be fair . . .

March is the month traditionally associated with strong winds and gales. These often result from large differences in temperature that can develop in the atmosphere between the residual cold air of winter and the advancing warmth generated by the sun as it moves northwards . . .

. . . 6th March 1967 winds up to 145 mph (232 kph) recorded in the Cairngorms, Scotland . . . 24th March 1986 winds reached 153 mph (245 kph) at a height of 1047m (3400ft) . . .

*

Cold March, Wet April and Hot May,
Will make a fruitful year they say . . .

*

A measure of March dust
is worth its weight in gold . . .

If the meadows grow in March,
plenty will follow . . .

25

A particularly Welsh proverb which suggests that a bright start to the month is likely to be followed by bad weather is . . .

> If the birds sing before St. David's Day
> They will be silent before Lady Day . . .

The corresponding dates are 1st March and 25th March.

*

A cold snap in late March is known as a . . .

> Blackthorn Winter . . .

March Snowfalls . . .

1886 and 1888	Severe easterly blizzards over North England and Scotland.
9 March 1891	Very heavy snow and gales over the southwest peninsula, especially Dartmoor. The so called 'Zulu Express' left Paddington at 3 pm Monday 9th and eventually arrived at Plymouth at 8.30 pm Friday 13th. It was trapped for four days near Brent, south Devon, but the plight of the passengers was not reported in the London Press until the 14th, due to the collapse of telegraph lines and the isolation of the southwest.
1901	Between the 20th and 29th an estimated 6ft (2m) of snow fell in North Wales.
1916	Severe snowstorms across England with estimated drifts of up to 40ft(12m) on Exmoor.
1937	Between 4th and 13th a persistent blizzard hit Ulster in Northern Ireland and five persons died.
1941	A great blizzard raged over Sutherland in Scotland and an estimated 30,000 sheep perished.
1947	After a particularly bitter winter more heavy snow fell on 4th giving severe drifting in southern England.
1952	Heavy snowfalls on 29th with 60 mph (100 kph) winds producing drifts. Northolt reported 10.5in (27cm).
1969	Snow fell during the first three weeks especially over north England.
1971	Five inches (12cm) of snow over Kent by 4th.

Some Notable March Weather . . .

2 March 1977	"Red rain" or Sahara dust falls widely reported over southern England.
4-6 March 1983	In 72hrs. 349mm (13.7in) of rain fell in Sutherland, Scotland.
9 March 1948	Temperature reached 23.3C (74F) at Kensington.
10 March 1947	Severe flooding in the Thames valley followed a rapid thaw.
14 March 1947	Temperature fell to minus 19.4C (– 3F) at Glenlivet, Scotland.
27 March 1968	Temperature of 25C (78F) at Mildenhall, Suffolk, a March record for UK.

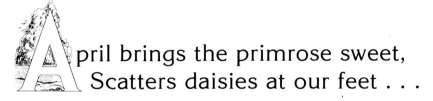

April brings the primrose sweet, Scatters daisies at our feet . . .

. . . the month of showers . . . immortalised in song . . .

*

A mild April will wet the bush and dry the bush . . .

. . . seems to be a reference to showers, which in weather forecasts can be described by any of the following:

light-; moderate-; heavy-; blustery-;
squally-; wintry-; thundery-;
-of hail; -of sleet; -of rain;
-in places; -at times; -here and there;
localised-; widespread-; frequent-; isolated-;

Not forgetting the good old standby:

. . . sunshine and showers . . . !

*

A dry April everything languishes . . .

. . . on average April is one of the driest months. For example in 1893 no significant rain fell over most of southern England and in 1982 only 6mm (¼in) was recorded at Wye College in Kent . . .

*

No blustering blasts from March need April borrow,
His own oft proves enough to breed us sorrow . . .

. . . on 23rd April 1947 wind speeds reached 99 mph (160 kph) and HMS Warspite was driven aground off the Cornish coast . . . on 3rd April 1949 gusts reached 70 mph (112 kph) in the Dover Strait . . . Easter Monday 1950 a wind of 92 mph (147 kph) was reported at Blackpool . . . at Yeovilton in Somerset on 12th April 1969 winds reached 80 mph (130 kph) . . .

*

Wet and warmth in April will cause the farmer to sing like a Nightingale . . .

Easter snow 1983

April Snowfalls . . .

1892 Heavy snowfall across Sussex and Kent produced up to 30cm (12in) at Rochester and 16cm (6½in) at Cranbrook.

1908 On the 24th up to 30cm (12in) fell over southern England and caused disruption to train travel.

1917 Early in the month very heavy snow showers affected the Cheviot Hills, causing the deaths of many lambs.

1919 North London and Essex had snow up to 38cm (15in) in depth on the 28th.

1948 Snowflakes up to 6cm (2½in) in diameter fell in the Midlands and parts of Wales early in the month.

1950 On the 25th snow stretched from Salisbury to Faversham and was up to 25cm (10in) in depth at Sanderstead, Surrey.

1958 An Easter snowstorm hit the Scottish Borders and by mid-month there were snow showers over Cornwall.

1966 Drifts up to 150cm (5ft) over northeast England by the end of the 2nd. On the 14th 12cm (5in) fell over the south.

1968 On the 2nd snow covered most of the United Kingdom.

1970 Snowfall reported in most places on the 3rd.

1975 Up to 15cm (6in) at Doddington, Kent.

1978 On the 10th snow fell in London and the southeast.

1981 Severe late wintry weather caused snow across much of the United Kingdom except the southwest. Heavy blizzards hit the Northeast, Midlands and Wales, during the period 23rd-26th.

1983 Kent received 10cm (4in) of snow on the 3rd.

Notable April Weather . . .

1 April 1967   Minimum temperature fell to minus 7C (2F) at Ross on Wye

2 April 1987   Total rainfall of 48mm (2in) at Okehampton, Devon in 24hrs.

16 April 1949 In an Easter heatwave temperatures reached 28C (82F).

ay brings flocks of little lambs, Skipping by their fleecy dams . . .

. . . In the North, west Scotland and Northern Ireland, May is on average the sunniest month of the year. In May 1946 sunshine was up to 90 hours above normal in Scotland but in London and the southeast it was 30 hours less than average.

In 1977, on the 27th, the temperature reached 27.9C(82F) in the Highlands of Scotland. On May 29 1944, it reached 32.8C(91F) in parts of Kent and Sussex.

Conversely, in 1935, 1961 and 1967 a severe late frost caused damage to blossom . . .

Rain constant in May, better away . . .

*

Flowers before May, as well away . . .

*

A cold May brings healthy days . . .

*

Our forefathers seemed not too bothered by low temperatures in May, probably because they did not grow fruit but concentrated on corn and hay, crops less susceptible to sudden drops in air temperatures . . .

Cold wind in May lessens not the crop . . .

*

Cold May, full barn . . .

*

A showery May, loaded land of corn and hay . . .

*

. . . In European folklore the 11th, 12th and 13th of May are dedicated to the Ice Saints . . .

One interesting saying connects the appearance of two full moons in May with wet weather . . .

Two full moons in May,
Bring rain for a year and a day . . .

. . . Two full moons occur in May, roughly every 19 years, most recent was in 1988. Obviously for this saying to be true it must be based on a 19 year weather cycle.

29

Examination of the rainfall in the period May to the following April for those years when two full moons occur gives the following results . . .

Hastings Rainfall May-April Inclusive
**Two full moons in May*

Year	Total(mm)		Year	Total(mm)	
1892/93	717		1949/50	710	
1893/94**	750	NO	1950/51**	855	YES
1894/95	862		1951/52	787	
1911/12	778		1968/69	656	
1912/13**	907	YES	1969/70**	810	YES
1913/14	768		1970/71	728	
1930/31	936		1978/88	1010	
1931/32**	669	NO	1988/89**	Estimated well below average	NO
1932/33	751				

These results show that the saying appears to have little evidence to support it. The long time scale between events (19 years) makes one wonder if this saying had its origins in 1913, when it was a particularly wet year. It is hard to imagine our forefathers having ready access to predictions of the full moon plus the appropriate rainfall figures, and even if they did they would have to remember the 19 year interval.

The saying also appears in other forms that relate two full moons in any month to the prospect of floods. Is there any basis to this idea . . . ?

Now at the time of a full moon, or a new moon, we get 'Spring Tides'.

The term 'Spring' in this context has nothing to do with the season, it means that the difference in water level between high and low tide is large.

Thus at the time of a Spring Tide the water moves further up and down the beach.

If the Spring Tide coincides with the arrival of very low pressure this can have the effect of markedly increasing the height at high water, giving coastal floods.

For example a drop in pressure of 34 millibars (1in) can increase the height of any tide by about 0.3m (1ft).

Since low pressure is often associated with strong winds, which can further whip up waves, it is easy to see that, in the right conditions, floods could occur around the time of a full moon, near the coast.

It is equally true of course for the new moon which is also responsible for Spring Tides.

Naturally any month with two full, or new, moons has a greater risk of flooding if the conditions are favourable.

Two full or new moons occur in any month about once every three years.

Therefore, sayings that connect this event with potential flooding do have some substance.

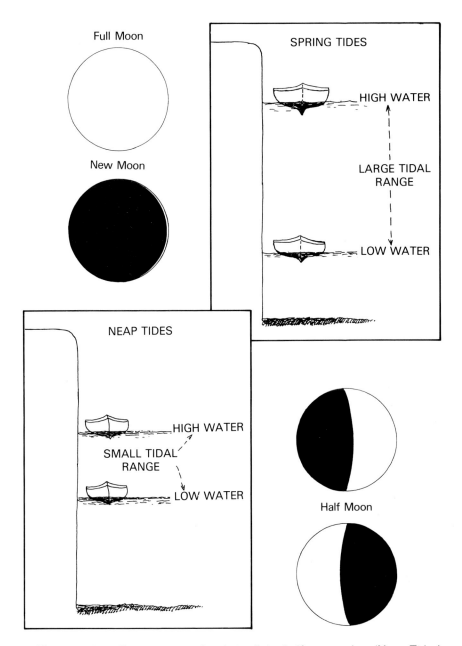

Full Moon

New Moon

SPRING TIDES

HIGH WATER

LARGE TIDAL RANGE

LOW WATER

NEAP TIDES

HIGH WATER

SMALL TIDAL RANGE

LOW WATER

Half Moon

The opposite effect occurs at the time of the half moon when 'Neap Tides' occur. This time there is only a small difference between the water level at high and low tides.

31

Dover Castle

May Snowfalls . . .

10 May 1943	After one of the mildest winters on record 1ft (30cm) of snow fell in the Pennines.
13 May 1886	Snow up to 25cm (10in) near Appleby, Cumbria and 18cm (7in) in Shropshire.
15 May 1923	Snowfall in the Cotswolds.
17 May 1955	Heavy snowfall in the Peak District and Pennines. Overnight snow in London did not settle.
18 May 1935	20cm (8in) of snow in South Devon and Cornwall. Golf at Southport cancelled because of snow. At the same time the east coast enjoyed continuous sunshine . . .
18 May 1891	Midlands and East Anglia hit by up to 15cm (6in) of snow.

Notable May Weather . . .

1 May 1948	15cm (6in) of hail in Berkshire.
11 May 1967	Rainfall total 55mm (2.2in) in Manchester in 24hrs.
12 May 1886	Over 60 hours of very heavy rain fell in the West Midlands.
20 May 1984	10cm (4in) of hail on M40 in Buckinghamshire.
20 May 1985	Thunderstorm at Brize Norton, Wilts., gave 51mm (2in) of rain in just two hours.
23 May 1966	Wind speed reached 100 mph (160 kph) in a gust over the Isle of Man.
31 May 1947	Temperature reached 32.7C (91F) in London.

une brings flowers like the roses, Fills children's hands with pretty posies . . .

. . . Over England and Wales June is usually the sunniest month. The average for the southeast of England is over 210 hours of sunshine, and in South Wales it is similar. In June 1975 Plymouth recorded over 300 hours of sunshine as did North Wales. Whilst in 1976 it was the turn of Lowestoft to break the '300' barrier. Towards the end of June that year temperatures of over 35C (95F) were reached in London and Southampton. However, in June 1975, on the 2nd, snowfall over the Pennines disrupted cricket in Derbyshire, and even got as far south as London . . .

*

Sunny June makes early rising reapers . . .

*

A rainy June makes the grass grow . . .

. . . on the 4th June 1982, at Cheshunt (Herts.) 92mm (almost 4in) of rain fell during a thunderstorm . . .

*

Sleep not in June, remember the frost of January . . .

*

If June be oft times wet and oft times dry,
Then merry will be the farmer's eye . . .

. . . the 'sunshine and showers' forecast which is probably good growing weather . . .

*

. . . Thunderstorms can cause crop damage because they can produce hailstones. On June 5th 1983 hailstones up to 30mm (1¼in) in size fell along the south coast . . .

Notable June Weather . . .

3 June 1948	River Derwent floods after 24hrs rain.
10 June 1948	Severe thunderstorms at Moor Park, Hertfordshire with 50mm (2in) of rain. A man is killed by lightning at London airport.
24 June 1982	66mm (2.6in) of rain in 24hrs at Chesterfield, Derbyshire.
26 June 1973	Tornado hits Cranfield, Bedfordshire causing structural damage.

34

. . . All on a summer's day . . .

 uly brings hopes of summer fun, Of scorching heat from flaming sun . . .

. . . Usually the warmest month of the year. In 1983 July was the warmest calendar month ever, with an average temperature of 19.2C (66.5F).

The highest temperature ever recorded in the United Kingdom was on 22nd July 1868 at Tonbridge, Kent, when a thermometer in the garden of Dr. George Fielding's house, reached somewhere close to 38C (100.5F).

In that year of 1868 from May to September the sun bore down from a cloudless sky with devastating effect. Dr Fielding recorded 66 days in the period when the temperature exceeded 27C (80F), 25 days when it exceeded 32C (90F) and six days when it went over 35C (95F). In the heatwave of 1976, 32C (90F) was exceeded on seven successive days at Cheltenham, Gloucesterhire, and 35C (95F) was topped only once.

At the end of the 1868 heatwave it is estimated that over 20,000 extra deaths were registered . . .

The English summer is three hot days followed by a thunderstorm . . .

*

. . . in July 1565 a terrific thunderstorm raged all night over London . . . and a similar event occurred during the night of 14 July 1945 . . .

*

. . . on the 27th and 28th July 1971, 118mm (over 4in) of rain fell across East Anglia due to thunderstorms . . .

35

. . . St Swithin's Day . . .

"This is the month of St Swithin's Day,
When if there be rain, then they do say:
'For forty days and nights it will,
More or less, some rain distil'"

July 15th is St Swithin's day and the belief of the saying is still well held, although the facts do nothing to support its truth, quite the contrary.

St Swithin, who died in 862, was a Bishop of Winchester. He was a particularly humble man, who left instructions that, after his death, he should be buried: 'Where he would be exposed to . . . the drops falling from above . . .'

However, well after his death it is alleged that he appeared in visions now asking that his bones be brought inside the church. Consequently, on July 15th 971, his remains were transferred from the churchyard into a jewel encrusted golden shrine inside the precincts of the church.

His title of 'Saint' is popularly ascribed since he was never officially canonized.

The origins of the connection between the weather and his day is a mystery.

Similar beliefs exist in other lands linking Saints' days to weather prediction.

Notable July Weather . . .

6 July 1983   73mm (3in) of rain fell in 20 minutes at Kew.
13 July 1983   Temperature of 33C (91F) at Cardiff.

In July 1948 there was a ground frost over parts of the south of England.

36

August is the time for fruit, And the sportsmen start to shoot . . .

If August be dry then many rejoice . . .

. . . fairly reasonable bearing in mind it's the time most people take their holidays . . .

*

There is a shortage of weather sayings for August, perhaps like us today our forefathers took a bit of a holiday!

The poet Byron does make the following observation in 'Don Juan':

"The English winter, ending in July,
to recommence in August . . ."

*

August can be a dry month, but on average it is the wettest of the summer months. Like July it is usually thunderstorms that cause the problems.

On the 15th August 1952 a small thundery low drifted slowly northwards across the English Channel from the Brittany peninsula. Severe thunderstorms developed over southern England and rainfall was very heavy over Devonshire, particularly Exmoor where over 200mm (8in) fell. Serious flooding was the result and the small town of Lynmouth was virtually destroyed with the loss of over 30 lives . . .

Notable August Weather . . .

6 August 1952	53mm (2.1in) of rain recorded in 30 minutes at Wembley Town Hall.
7 August 1973	Tornado hits Thorpe Bay and Foulness in Essex leaving a trail of damage.
9 August 1911	Temperature reaches 37C (98F), one of the highest recorded in the UK.
25-26 August 1912	Over 180mm (7in) of rain brought severe floods to Norwich.

Thunderstorms . . .

The summer months of June, July and August are always likely to produce violent thunderstorms.

Such storms rely on strong surface heating to trigger them and the near continent is a favourite breeding ground. After starting their development they often drift across the short channel crossing to affect south east Kent, from where the following originates . . .

> If the wind increases and blows towards a distant thunderstorm then the storm will approach, but if the wind blows outwards from the storm then expect it to move away . . .

Having developed over France the thunderclouds can drift towards the south coast on light southerly winds present in the upper levels of the atmosphere.

As they approach a place the tremendous updraughts in the clouds tend to make the winds near the the surface flow towards the base of the cloud.

Thus with the cloud to the south the winds now tend to be from the north at the surface, and yet the storm continues to advance because it is moved by the upper southerly flow . . .

When the storm is very near, especially once the rain or hail has started, then very severe winds can gust downwards and outwards from the base of the cloud.

Summer thunderstorms are usually active in the late afternoon or early evening, because it takes time for the sun to heat the ground and the convection to get going.

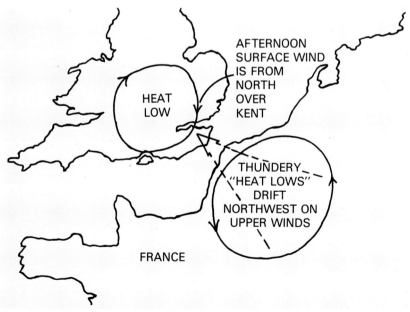

AFTERNOON
SURFACE WIND
IS FROM
NORTH
OVER
KENT

HEAT
LOW

THUNDERY
"HEAT LOWS"
DRIFT
NORTHWEST ON
UPPER WINDS

FRANCE

Summer Thunderstorm . . .

Róger Nicholson

Sheet lightning and forked lightning . . .

There is really no difference between the two. So called Sheet lightning is caused by the diffusing effect of the cloud, whereas Forked lightning occurs in clear air.

Lightning strokes can be inside clouds (Sheet), between clouds (Forked or Sheet if a cloud is in the way) and between cloud and surface (Forked). When lightning damages property we often say a 'Thunderbolt' has struck.

Thunder is the noise made by the lightning stroke. Have you ever noticed the crackling sounds that can be heard as you remove a nylon sweater or shirt? Those crackles are caused by tiny sparks of static electricity formed by the nylon rubbing against other material or your hair, especially if it is dry.

They are just like miniature thunderstorms. If you stand in a totally dark room and wait a few minutes for your eyes to adjust to the dark and then remove a nylon sweater you might be amazed at the display from the sparks of static electricity.

To tell how far away a thunderstorm is you must start counting as soon as you see a flash of lightning. Count slowly, try to guess the seconds, a useful way of doing this is to say . . 'ONE thousand . . TWO thousand . . THREE thousand . . etc . .' which gives about three seconds.

Keep the count going until you hear the thunder and the rule is . . .

> For each six seconds between the flash and the noise of the thunder the storm is about one mile away . . . it is equal to about 3½ seconds for each kilometre . . .

eptember sees the harvest home Fills the barns with wheat and corn . . .

. . . the second week of September is one of the driest of the year in central and eastern England . . .

*

Dry mild September gives cellars full of good ale . . .

. . . an obvious reference to the hop harvest . . .

*

September is the month of the equinox when the sun leaves the northern hemisphere.

It is a time when once again the weather can be extreme as is recognised by the saying:

September can break bridges or dry up the ditches . . .

From 1973 to 1976 there was a run of very wet Septembers, especially in the south:

Place	Wye (Kent)	Kew	Plymouth	Aberdeen
Ave. Rain mm(in)	63 (2.5)	50 (1.9)	73 (2.9)	67 (2.6)
1973	182 (7.2)	71 (2.8)	70 (2.8)	103 (4.2)
1974	141 (5.6)	124 (4.9)	181 (7.2)	70 (2.8)
1975	119 (4.7)	120 (4.7)	98 (3.9)	88 (3.5)
1976	148 (5.8)	107 (4.2)	148 (5.8)	173 (6.8)

Now there is a saying that goes . . .

Wet September, Dry May . . .

Of course this can easily be tested by study of rainfall records, and for the places shown the totals for the following May are:

Place	Wye (Kent)	Kew	Plymouth	Aberdeen
Ave. Rain mm(in)	50 (1.9)	46 (1.8)	61 (2.4)	71 (2.8)
1974	15 (0.6)	25 (0.9)	81 (3.2)	45 (1.8)
1975	71 (2.8)	67 (2.6)	41 (1.6)	35 (1.3)
1976	19 (0.7)	22 (0.9)	38 (1.5)	48 (1.9)
1977	49 (1.9)	36 (1.4)	67 (2.6)	87 (3.4)
Results	2 Dry	3 Dry	2 Dry	3 Dry

A better idea of the truth of this saying can be obtained by examining data for a longer time scale.

Rainfall records for Hastings go back to 1875 and picking out Septembers when the total rain was 1½ time or more than the average gives 27 occasions.

Looking at the rainfall totals for the subsequent May it was found that:

On 14 occasions May was dry
on only four occasions it was average
and on nine occasions it was definitely wet

Analysing over 50 years date from Wye (Kent) gives the following results:

There were 13 occasions when the September rainfall was 1½ times or more than average.

Of the subsequent 13 Mays the totals divided as follows:

On seven occasions it was dry
on four occasions it was average
on only two occasions it was definitely wet

Thus on the basis of this very limited analysis it seems there might be some truth in the saying . . . but of course it does not work every year!

*

As old as the moon be on Michaelmas Day,
As many days after then floods come, they say . . .

. . . Michaelmas Day is September 29th . . .

In 1987 the moon was seven days old on September 29th and seven days later on October 7th, heavy flooding occurred in parts of Kent . . .

However, in 1988 the moon was 18 days old on Michaelmas Day but 18 days later there was no flooding, in fact October was quite a dry month comparatively . . .

*

A warm settled spell in late September is known as an 'Old Wives Summer' . . .

In September 1941 only 4mm (0.1in) of rain fell over Kent, and in 1959 a similar amount was recorded.

On September 2nd 1906 a temperature of 35.6C (96F) was reached in south Yorkshire . . .

From the 14th to 16th September 1968 rainfall of over 200mm (8in) was recorded in the southeast with consequent severe flooding . . .

Tonbridge High Street, September 16th 1968

Storm damage, October 16th 1987

ctober and the nights grow long,
And the winds are often strong...

... On the night of 15/16th October 1987 the winds reached 100 mph (160 kph) in gusts across southern England.

It was the night of the 'Great Storm' and millions of pounds worth of damage was done to homes and other buildings. An estimated 15 million trees were blown down that night.

The storm struck after a period of particularly heavy rain which softened the soil around the tree roots. Also the winds changed direction dramatically as the storm centre moved rapidly northwards and the trees were in full canopy, thus receiving the full force of the violent gusts, as pressure rose very rapidly . . .

The barograph trace for the week of the Great Storm shows how the pressure changed as the storm moved across the South . . .

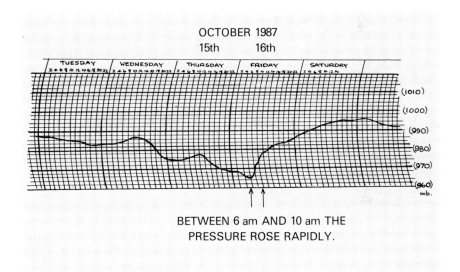

OCTOBER 1987
15th   16th

BETWEEN 6 am AND 10 am THE
PRESSURE ROSE RAPIDLY.

Following that disaster the weathermen were criticised for not forecasting the severity of the winds and to some extent it is justified.

Even if the forecast had been accurate it is difficult to imagine what action could have been taken to avoid the considerable damage, much of which was due to falling trees.

45

Autumn leaves after the storm

My forecast was for Gales and this was the picture chosen for the final summary. Sent in by Leanne Busbridge of Sittingbourne, it proved very appropriate!

Because of the extensive damage it caused, that particular storm has had a major impact on the population in the south of England, but looking back at just a few of the records of the last 40 years shows that in October severe gales are not uncommon . . .

On the 3rd 1967, gusts up to 80 mph (130 kph) at Portland Bill . . .

14th 1976, wind speeds reached 108 mph (173 kph) at Prawle Point, Devon . . .

15th 1983, severe gales along the Channel with gusts up to 88 mph (140 kph) over the Isle of Wight . . .

16th 1967, up to 100 mph (160 kph) winds recorded at Whitby, Yorkshire . . .

16/17th 1948, overnight severe gales uprooted trees in central London and the south east . . .

19th 1970 Gusts up to 92 mph (147 kph) near Stirling as storms hit Scotland . . .

20th 1949 Gusts to 81 mph (131 kph) at Shoeburyness in Essex . . .

21st 1973 over 100 mph (160 kph) reported from Flamborough Head . . .

23rd 1949 severe southerly gales damage sea wall at Folkestone and property along the south coast . . .

23rd 1972 Wind speeds up to 82 mph (132 kph) in Shetland . . .

28th 1974 severe gales lash the whole country . . .

30th 1986 maximum wind at Cairngorm of 143 mph (229 kph) . . .

It is interesting to note that a wind speed of 60 mph exerts a force of 10 pounds per square foot, whilst at just over 80 mph the force is doubled to 20 pounds per square foot.

In metric units at a wind speed of 100 kph the force is 50 kg per square metre and at 130 kph it doubles to 100 Kg per square metre.

The storm has wrongly been called a 'Hurricane'; strictly it was not. The reason for the misnomer is that winds often exceeded 'Hurricane Force'.

This means that they were above 64 knots (70 mph) on the Beaufort wind scale.

In meteorology the term 'Hurricane' refers to a 'Tropical Revolving Storm' and they are to be found in the West Indies or along the Pacific coast of central and north America.

In other parts of the world 'Tropical Revolving Storms' are known by other names, but they are all the same weather feature and can create the same amount of havoc.

Part of World	Name	Season
West Indies East North Pacific	Hurricane	June to November
West Pacific	Typhoon	July to November
Indian Ocean (North)	Cyclone	June to November
North Australia Coast South Indian Ocean	Cyclone	December to April

Nowadays, more and more people are taking holidays in the West Indies and for predicting the worst months for hurricanes the following rhyme is worth remembering:

June, probably too soon,
July, you're on standby,
August, keep a look out you must,
September, the month to remember,
October, probably over . . .

. . . but hurricanes can occur in November and the one of 1932 was particularly severe . . .

*

St Luke's little summer . . .

. . . St Luke's day is October 18th and fine warm spell around that time is referred to by this name.

In the USA such a settled spell is known as an 'Indian summer' since it was traditionally the time the tribes harvested their corn.

The weather pattern often has a settled look at about this time with high pressure near the British Isles.

Towards the end of the month the weather is often much more stormy and wet.

Recent October warm spells:

9th (1969)	27C (80F) at Liphook, Hants
16th (1977)	23C (73F) at Valley, Anglesey
11th (1978)	25C (77F) over eastern England
1st (1985)	28.4C (83F) at Cranwell, Lincs.

*

and snowfalls . . .

27th (1950)	over Dorset, Somerset and Gloucs.
13th (1971)	sleet and snow over the Midlands and South Wales
28th (1974)	3ft of snow closed the Perth to Braemar road

ovember oft brings an autumn lull,
With clammy fogs that make it
dull . . .

. . . the third week in November is on average one of the foggiest of the year in the south and east of England . . .

Between the 4th and 6th of November 1901 a dense fog settled on London and there were many fatalities as a result . . .

The dense fogs that were a feature of London and other major cities became known as 'Smogs' because the smoke from commercial and domestic chimneys added vast amounts of pollutants and chemical irritants to the atmosphere. This caused bronchial problems and because of the slightly greenish tinge to the fog, they became known as 'Pea soupers'.

The problem was virtually eliminated by the 'Clean Air Act'.

Fog . . . always a hazard to driving . . .

St. Martin's Summer . . .

November 11th is St. Martin's day and a spell of warm weather around this date is known by this name.

It is mentioned in Shakespeare's 'Henry VI':

"Expect St. Martin's summer halcyon days . . ."

Halcyon is the Greek for Kingfisher and the ancients believed that the Kingfisher laid and incubated its eggs on the surface of the sea for fourteen days before the winter solstice. Obviously over this period the sea was very calm.

On the 10th in 1977 the temperature in central London reached 18C (65F) . . .

At Prestatyn, North Wales on 4th November 1948 a temperature of 22C (71F) was recorded.

November is usually a wet month . . .

. . . on 11th 1929, 211mm (8.3in) of rain fell in the Rhondda Valley, South Wales, in 24 hours

. . . on 6th 1951, at Dyce, Aberdeen, 92mm (3.6in) was recorded in 36 hours . . .

. . . on 20th 1965 up to 76mm (3in) fell at Brighton.

The wettest November at Hastings since 1875 was in 1926, when 208mm (8.2in) fell . . .

When November ice will hold a duck,
then winter will be mild with muck . . .

. . . Cold spells are not uncommon in November.

In 1947 on the 30th November the minimum temperature was minus 10C (14F) at Yeovilton and that subsequent winter was very mild and stormy apart from the week 21st to 28th February 1948, when up to 30cm (1ft) of snow fell in the southeast. Even the Scilly Isles had 5cm (2in) of snow and in Guernsey it was 15cm (6in).

On the 15th November 1965 day maximum temperatures did not rise above freezing point. The winter that followed was mostly mild and wet, apart from a wintry spell in mid-January 1966, which brought 30cm (1ft) of snow to parts of Kent on the 15th . . .

Study of weather records suggest that when a mild November is followed by a mild December, then the winter will probably remain mild.

The next saying comes from East Anglia and seems to go against what the records suggest:

If a tree shows buds in November,
the winter will last until May . . .

Some November Snowfalls

18th (1947)   Snow from Bristol to London
22nd (1965)   Extensive snowfall in the south
17th (1969)   Snow in Surrey and the south east
18th (1972)   Snow over the Downs . . . up to 20cm (8in) on Dartmoor.
4/6th (1980)   Up to 6cm (2½in) over southern England and in the Channel Isles.
19th (1985)   4cm (1½in) in the Maidstone area (Kent).
19th (1988)   10cm (4in) fell around Dover and Folkestone.

One Sattorday Nov: 27th 1703 about one aclock in the morning arose a great storme of wind — wch continued fill six wth that violence that itt destroyd eleaven of his — Majestyes ships of war (wth most of the men belonging to them) one our owne costs. Besides a great number of Merchant men; and did vast damage att land to horses and cattle. above 20 peeple were kild by ye fale of stacks of chimleys in London. as alsew ye Bishop of Bath & Wells and his lady were kiled in their bed together in ye Country as alsew ye Lady Penelope sister to ye Bishop of London was kiled in hir bead. my nephew Francis Drinkwater was lost in one of his Majestyes fore said ships, ye Newcastle and above two hundred more of the men belonging to thatt ship — it began ssw e varied ofton to sw e westy by north — for wch a fast was kept one monsday Jan 19th 170¾ through out England.

Severe gales are not uncommon . . .

. . . in November 1785 a Tornado struck Nottingham, causing much damage to property and livestock . . .

. . . 13th 1959 winds of up to 105 mph (168 kph) at the Lizard, Cornwall . . .

. . . 1st 1965, 75 mph (120 kph) in the North with gusts of up to 117 mph (187 kph) in Larnarkshire . . .

. . . at Flamborough Head gust of 98 mph (157 kph) on the 16th 1966 . . .

. . . between the 2nd and 4th 1970 severe gales hit the country and a gust of 143 mph (229 kph) was recorded at Snaefell on the Isle of Man, while at Cairngorm ski lift the maximum was 115 mph (184 kph) . . .

. . . on the 29th 1976 a gust of 110 mph (176 kph) hit the Needles on the Isle of Wight . . .

. . . at Fair Isle on the 15th 1978 the top gust reached 115 mph (185 kph) . . .

The Great Storm that hit the English Channel and south coast on November 27th 1703 was particularly severe, rivalling that of October 1987.

It is estimated that as many as 6000 people may have lost their lives. There was much damage to property as well as loss of shipping at sea and livestock ashore.

The contemporary account, found inside an old bible describes just a small part of the tragedy . . .

The name alongside this account is 'Dr Kiddo' and what he said in modern idiom is:

"On Saturday November 27th 1703, about one o'clock in the morning arose a great storm of wind, which continued until six, with such violence that it destroyed eleven of His Majesty's ships of war (with most of the men belonging to them) on our own coasts. Besides a great number of merchantmen; and it did vast damage overland to horses and cattle. Over 20 people were killed by the fall of chimney stacks in London, as well as the Bishop of Bath and Wells and his lady who were killed in their bed in their country house. Also Lady Penelope, sister of the Bishop of London was killed in her bed. My nephew Francis Drinkwater was lost in one of His Majesty's ships, the 'Newcastle' together with over two hundred of the crew. It began in the south-southwest and veered later to southwest, then west by north. As a result a fast was kept on Monday January 19th 1704 throughout England".

. . . a hunting we shall go . . .

Stan Rycroft

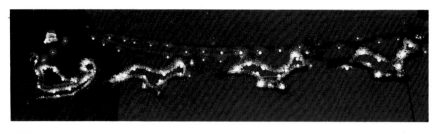

 ecember and we hope for snow,
At Christmas time, like long ago ...

The traditional Christmas is now a particularly rare event and yet we have the image strong in the national consciousness, no doubt because of the annual reinforcement from the pictures on our Christmas cards.

But why do we no longer enjoy snow or frosty weather around Christmas when our forefathers seemed to be guaranteed it?

The reason is quite simple and nothing to do with ideas like the so called 'Greenhouse effect theory' which suggests that the carbon dioxide released into our atmosphere, as a result of burning fossil fuels, might be helping to increase the average air temperature, thus making snow less likely.

It is largely due to the fact that we now celebrate Christmas Day earlier than they did in the past.

Before 1752, when a new calendar was introduced, Christmas Day occurred 11 days later than it does today.

Before 1752 Christmas Day was on what is now January 5th, and this fact is very significant in view of the type of weather that prevails across England.

Very dramatic changes can occur with large falls in temperature between late December and early January.

Thus you can see that before 1752, there was a much greater chance of cold weather, hence snow, affecting southern England at what was then their Christmas time.

Old ideas die hard . . .

A decidedly cold December is likely to be followed by three cold months . . .

. . . 1981 saw a very cold December with temperatures falling to minus 25C (− 13F) at Shawbury during the night of the 12th and during the day they reached only minus 12C (11F) as a maximum.

January 1982 saw record low temperatures and there were some very cold spells in the late February.

Christmas Snow

London saw significant snowfalls in 1906, 1927 and 1938, and a severe frost in 1939 allowed skating on frozen ponds over the holiday period.

In 1963 heavy snow started on Boxing Day and heralded one of the worst winters on record.

On Christmas Eve 1968 rain turned to snow over much of Wales and England to be followed by heavy snow over eastern areas between the 26th and 29th.

On Boxing Day 1970 20cm(8in) fell on the North Downs.

In 1976 there were some snow showers on Christmas Day mainly in the north and east.

Snow that fell in the week before Christmas in 1981 persisted through the festive period in many places.

*

If it snows on Christmas night,
Then the hop harvest 'twill be alright . . .

*

A green Christmas makes a fat churchyard . . .

. . . we've seen this one already with January in place of Christmas.

*

If on Christmas Day there's much wind in the air,
Then lots of fruit the orchards will bear . . .

December can be stormy, in 1703 a fierce gale blew down the Eddystone lighthouse on the night of the 7/8th. In 1879 a storm on the 28th caused the Tay Bridge disaster . . .

On the 15th in 1979 winds of 100 mph (160 kph) were measured at Lizard (Cornwall), Prawle Point (Devon) and the Needles (Isle of Wight) . . .

On 14/15th December 1986 a very deep depression between Greenland and Iceland was reckoned to have a central pressure below 920mb making it the lowest barometric pressure known in the North Atlantic . . .

Too cold for snow . . .

This is often true. Very cold air reaches us from the east and so it tends to be very dry. If the air is very dry there is not much chance of thick clouds developing and hence the risk of snow is reduced.

However, if thick clouds can develop *above* the very cold air near the surface, as described in the January weather pattern earlier, then heavy snowfall is possible.

Chatham Hill, January 1987

57

January 1987 . . . Somewhere in Kent . . .

Also, if the very cold air has a longish track across a relatively warm North Sea, then shower clouds can build up which precipitate snow on the east coast.

When air temperatures are very low, any snow that does fall will tend to be dry and powdery so that in moderate winds drifting can occur.

At other times when the temperature is not far below freezing at the surface, the snow tends to be 'sticky' so drifting requires very strong winds.

This is summed up in the following . . .

When snow falls dry, it means to lie,
But flakes light and soft bring rain oft . . .

A good example in recent years occurred over the weekend January 10th/11th 1987 across Kent.

Temperatures fell quickly as Siberian air arrived on the Saturday night so that by Monday up to 70cm (2½ft) of snow had fallen on the Isle of Sheppey as a result of showers that developed over the North Sea.

Maximum temperatures that day were around minus 10C (14F) but winds were quite light.

On the night of the 14th further snowfall plus gale force southeast winds caused drifts up to 5m (15ft) along the A20 between Maidstone and Ashford.

By the Saturday, milder air had returned and a thaw set in . . .

58

Animal antics . . .

There is a very strong theme in weather lore based on the assumption that animals and plants have some prognostic ability not held by man.

Consequently there is a large collection of sayings, many of which upon examination say the same thing but merely change the plant or animal.

The following are a small selection, starting with . . .

The Birds . . .

It seems that just about every 'chirrup', 'cheep', 'hoot', 'cluck' or 'screech' uttered by birds has some significance for forecasting the weather, or so our forefathers would have us believe . . .

If the Woodpecker sets low on the tree
Then sun and warmth there's sure to be . . .

It is also suggested that if the sounds of the woodpecker can be clearly heard even though it is far away, that this is a sign of rain to come.

And it is not only the woodpecker but the wise old owl, blackbird and even the cuckoo are all attributed with weather forecasting abilities . . .

If the old owl's hoot is heard quite plain,
Then it's a sign it's sure to rain . . .

When the Blackbird sings in the morning
Expect rain . . .

Cuckoo in the low land
Means rain is close at hand
But when he's high in the heather
Means we'll have fair weather . . .

The transmission of sounds over long distances in certain weather conditions has already been discussed . . .

The behaviour of birds also brings forth much comment . . .

When the Swallows fly high
Then it will remain dry
If the Swallows fly low
Standby for a blow . . .

It is probable that the high flying is a result of the birds chasing insects that have been lifted to greater than normal heights because of convection in hot dry weather. Whereas when they operate near the ground the conditions are less favourable, with stronger winds.

It is said that if rooks build their nests in the topmost branches of tall trees then the summer will be a good one.

There is a rookery near my home and it appears that the nests remain at the same height from year to year, and the rooks merely reoccupy them in the spring.

59

Four Legged Friends . . .

Cows lying down are said to indicate that rain is on the way.

I have never found this belief particularly reliable because in my experience, cows often seem to lie down because they fancy a rest!

However, I was told that there is a reason for this belief by a man I met once in a Pub.

He said that the lining of one of the cow's four stomachs was very susceptible to changes in atmospheric humidity. When the humidity was high then the cow suffered discomfort and to reduce this, had to lie down.

Humidity usually increases with the approach of rain so perhaps there is some truth in the idea after all . . .

"Nice day for a doze . . ."

While cats are attributed with the ability to forecast the coming weather . . .

When the cat washes behind her ears
Rain is on the way . . .

Cats sharpening their claws on trees or posts
Indicate windy weather . . .

. . . the dog does not appear to have any habit that is linked with the weather.

Peter Smith

If the squirrel many nuts do hoard,
Then winter will strike like a sword . . .

*

In bygone times asses and donkeys were much more in evidence than nowadays when they have been replaced by the motor car. Needless to say they were accorded predictive properties . . .

When you hear the
asses bray
There will be some rain
today . . .

If donkeys hang their ears
forward and downward
Then rain is close at hand . . .

"Is that rain I hear . . . ?"

61

Frogs

There is a belief that if you see a dark coloured frog then rain is on the way.

This idea may have some truth in it because a frog's skin contains a dark pigment. Now the skin itself responds to changes in atmospheric humidity. If the air is dry and hot, then the cells containing the pigment become small and so the frog appears lighter in colour. On the other hand if the conditions become wet and cold then the area of dark pigment spreads, thus the frog takes on a dark appearance.

> When the yellow frog turns to green,
> The cold and rain will soon be seen . . .

*

> Croaking frogs in spring,
> Will three times be frozen in . . .

*

> If a frog makes noise in the time of rain
> It will soon be warm and dry again . . .

*

. . . the following would imply the opposite . . .

> The louder the frog, the more the rain . . .

*

There is some ambiguity about the first part of the next saying; does it mean that the drought already exists? . . .

> When frogs spawn in the middle of the water,
> It is a sure sign of drought . . .

The second part makes a definite forecast . . .

> (When frogs spawn) . . . At the side it foretells a wet summer . . .

Bees

. . . There is a strong belief that the bee, especially the honey bee is a good indicator of deteriorating weather conditions.

Certainly bees on the wing are very susceptible to rain and heavy rain can kill them.

The saying . . .

> When many bees enter the hive and none leave,
> Then rain is at hand . . .

is another that has some merit.

The behaviour of the bees may be a result of the overall rise in humidity plus change in direction and increase in wind speed that often precedes rain or the decrease in light level as cloud cover increases.

Time to go home . . . ?

Other, less attractive creatures used in weather forecasting . . .

Fleas

. . . not the sort of weather aid most people would choose. It is said that when they are biting eagerly, it is a sign of rain.

It occurred to me that the dog owners might get some value from this by watching how often the dog was scratching!

Gnats

. . . are perhaps more familiar and the suggestion is that they are more active if rain is on the way . . . On the other hand if they dance in swarms at sunset then expect a fine day . . .

Leeches

. . . these aquatic animals if kept in a bottle of water are said to respond to weather changes. If the leech remained at the bottom then settled weather was expected. If moved slowly to the top then a change to bad weather was on the way. If it kept moving rapidly through the water then windy weather was due. First get your leech . . .!

Ants

. . . Most sayings seem to connect their activity with the onset of rain, but it seems that before the flying ants can leave the nest the humidity and temperature must be high. In summer such meteorological conditions are forerunners of thunderstorms . . .

Spiders

. . . On the east coast of England amongst the fishing folk is the belief that if cobwebs appear in the rigging of a boat at sea, it is a portent of fine weather. There are also farmers who associate the appearance of gossamer, which is spiders' web, floating in the air with a fine dry spell.

The explanation is that in the late summer or early autumn sunny calm weather provokes the small spiders into producing lots of fine thread on the surface of the grass. At dawn after a heavy dew this thread is clearly seen. As the day advances the sun dries out the threads and convection lifts them into the air. While airborne they become entangled and gossamer is produced. These threads can be wafted long distances by light winds, even out to sea where they become caught up in the ship's rigging.

The presence of a southeast breeze is particularly associated with this phenomenon. In autumn, over the east coast, a southeast airflow results from a region of high pressure centred over Germany, and high pressure at that time of the year often persists for several days . . .

Snails

. . . In Holland in the early 1950's there was a gentleman who claimed that he could get accurate long range forecasts of the winter to come by studying the behaviour of Roman Snails . . .

Trees of Knowledge . . .?

The early appearance, or otherwise, of certain buds and flowers, and the abundance of fruit or berries all have their place in weather lore.

Some of the best known include . . .

Oak before Ash
Only a splash
Ash before Oak
Sure of a soak . . .

Now it may be that you know
a version which says the exact opposite, because
in certain parts of the country such versions exist.

So depending upon where you live, you take your pick.

The idea that plenty of berries in the autumn is a predictor of a severe winter to come is not very reliable in my experience. It seems to mean that the previous spring and summer were quite good, plus the fact that the autumn was free of severe frosts, with the result that the birds were able to continue to eat worms and the like without having to raid the storehouse of the berries, as they have to do when heavy frosts occur over several days and the worms go deep into the soil.

Probably the best known combination is that of the Fir cone and Seaweed . . .

Certainly pine cones open and close in response to changes in atmospheric moisture content so hung out of doors they could give an indication of wet weather ahead.

In a similar way if the seaweed is collected from the shore and hung in a sheltered place outside, then as it dries it will be covered with a layer of salt.

Now salt responds quickly to changes in humidity and the seaweed itself becomes pliable when damp and rather brittle when dry. Thus this lowly plant could be a useful indicator of changes in the airstream and hence the weather pattern.

65

There is a group of plants whose flowers close up their petals when the sky grows dark. Amongst them are 'Livingstone Daisies' or Mesembryantheum and the 'Scarlet Pimpernel'.

The Pimpernel . . .

> To the weather the pimpernel is true
> It opens to the skies of blue
> But when it closes its bright red flower
> You can expect a passing shower . . .

The Onion . . .

> When the onion's skin is very thin
> Then a mild winter is coming in
> But if the onion skin is thick and tough
> Then winter will be cold and rough . . .

. . . it's enough to make you cry . . .!

Modern Weather Lore . . .

All the sayings and beliefs developed by our forefathers relating to weather prediction were the results of observation of their environment and the impact changes had on their daily lives.

Nowadays life is very different. I have already commented on its insularity and the increased distance between us and our environment when compared with our predecessors.

So is there any basis for us to continue to develop weather lore? Is there anything in our daily lives that can be an indicator of impending weather conditions? Surprisingly, I think there is . . .

There's always the media forecasts, of course, they are short term and the weather lore that seems to be associated with them runs along the lines . . . .

They never get it right . . .
They always get it wrong . . .

The first statement is strictly true. When you consider all the different elements that go to making up the weather forecast and the large areas that are covered, it is unlikely that, say, the temperature or wind speed will be exactly as forecast for the whole of the period. Most of the time they are reasonably right.

Looking at the second statement, if it has any truth then a really intelligent person could derive some value from such a forecast, simply by taking the opposite of what is predicted they could glean much useful information . . .

Then there are the radio and television themselves, they respond to differing weather conditions.

The radio signal suffers crackles when there is lightning around, especially on what I call 'Long wave' (200 khz). The closer and more active the storm, the louder and more persistent the crackles. Useful perhaps if you are travelling along a motorway at night because you can anticipate the possible torrential rain or even hail . . .

Television signals are susceptible to interference from foreign stations. This usually happens when the pressure is high. In the south east of England and along the south coast, interference from French and Belgian stations can occur when pressure is very high and light south east or south winds prevail.

When such interference exists it suggests that settled weather is indicated. In winter it would mean a cold spell perhaps.

A motor car parked outside on a clear night will cool quickly so that any water vapour in the air will tend to condense on it. Heavy condensation could be an indication of fog formation, especially in low lying areas or river valleys. For this to happen the wind must be very light.

If ice has formed on the car, then frost is likely, if it is not already occuring.

67

Contrails

Aircraft condensation trails, those long white streaks that appear high in the sky can be useful indicators of a change in the weather pattern.

If they are long, persistent and tend to spread outwards then it indicates that rain is on the way.

On the other hand if they are short and quickly disappear, it indicates rising pressure and settled weather.

Have you noticed that on occasions you tend to suffer lots of little electric shocks, possibly from car doors or even from the cat when you go to stroke it!

The presence of these means that the air is very dry, and in such conditions in winter a severe frost is possible. At the same time pressure is probably high so a settled spell is likely.

Many homes these days have a barometer and careful study of the way the pressure rises and falls can lead to good forecasts.

One of the best known pieces of modern weather lore concerns the so called BUCHAN'S PERIODS . . .

Alexander Buchan was a Scotsman and an eminent meteorologist and in 1869 he carried out a statistical analysis of weather data for Scotland.

From this he identified certain periods when it was likely to be cold and others when it was more likely to be warm.

Not unexpectedly there are more cold periods than warm . . .

First cold period	last 18 days in February
Second cold period	11th to 14th April
Third cold period	9th to 14th May
Fourth cold period	29th June to 4th July
Fifth cold period	6th to 11th August
Sixth cold period	6th to 13th November
First warm period	12th to 15th July
Second warm period	12th to 15th August

Although the data is for Scotland the ideas have spread to other parts of the country.

A much more detailed analysis of weather data gathered over more than 50 years showed that at certain times during the year there was a much greater chance of certain weather patterns prevailing than at other times. From these results the following conclusions can be drawn for the south of England . . .

Month	Weather Pattern	Average Dates (Start-Finish)
January	Stormy	8th to 17th
	Stormy	24th to 31st
February	Settled (cold?)	8th to 16th
	Cold spell	21st to 25th
Feb/March	Stormy	26th to 9th March
March	Stormy	24th to 31st
June	Warm period	12th to 17th
July	Warm period	10th to 24th
August	Stormy	24th to 28th
September	Settled (Warm)	1st to 16th
	Stormy	17th to 24th
October	Stormy	5th to 12th
	Settled (Warm)	16th to 20th
November	Settled	15th to 20th
	Stormy	24th to 14th Dec
December	Settled	14th to 21st
	Stormy	26th to 29th

From this table we could perhaps start to plan the year ahead, selecting the best dates for holidays and so on. Unfortunately there is no guarantee that any year will follow this pattern, which all makes for an interesting life at least.

The greater incidence of 'stormy' compared with 'settled' says a lot about our climate.

*

Buys Ballot's Law

In the northern hemisphere if you stand with your back to the wind then LOW pressure is on the LEFT.

Obviously then HIGH pressure is on the RIGHT.

In the southern hemisphere the situation is the reverse.

This means that, for the south of England, an east wind means high pressure to the north and low pressure to the south . . .

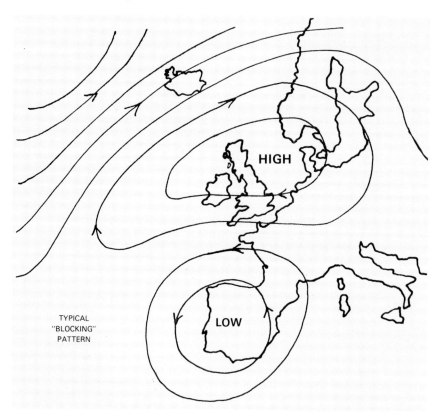

TYPICAL
"BLOCKING"
PATTERN

Blocking Patterns

Study of the pressure maps presented on TV and in some newspapers, plus a look at the barometer to see how the pressure is changing, can sometimes give clues to long range forecasts.

By long range I mean up to three days ahead.

The pattern to look for is of a HIGH centred near the United Kingdom and a LOW to the south, over Iberia or the western Mediterranean.

If you see such a pattern and it lasts for THREE days then it will probably last for a further TWO to FOUR days, that is up to a total of seven days.

If the pattern persists for a total of seven days it will probably last for a further FOUR days, making a total of eleven.

Beyond this reckon on about three days until a change.

In winter such systems can give bitterly cold weather in the south (see January), whilst in the autumn it can be the 'Indian Summer'.